Speech

for kids

Speech Sounds and Language
Development:

Delay or Disorder?

Helpful Games and Therapy Ideas
from a Speech and Language Therapist
for Parents to Try at HOME

Speech and Language Therapist

Yasmin Akhtar

Speech Therapy for Kids

Yasmin Akhtar

Acknowledgment

I would like to take this opportunity to say a HUGE thank you to all the amazing parents in my Facebook group, 'Kids delayed speech and language support group' who have been supporting me and my journey as a self-Publishing author.

Thank you to my Special 6 Mums/Moms and kids!! for taking part in the Makaton Signs Project and sending in the photos – I am honoured that I get to be part of the story you will tell your children when they are older of how they had their photos in a book which is helping lots of parents and children. see chapter 8 for our beautiful/handsome models!!

Yasmin Akhtar

Contents

Contents

Yasmin Akhtar

Yasmin Akhtar

A Gift for you!

As we all know, children with ASD learn better with visual aids, I have created a step-by-step potty-training strip with words and pictures, which you can stick on the bathroom wall or your living room or both!

The steps include:

- **Pulling down each item of clothing**
- **Sitting on the potty**
- **Pulling all clothes up**
- **Emptying the potty into the toilet**
- **Washing hands**

These step-by-step instructions will make it easier and fun to explain/show to your child.

To access this FREE resource, pleas click the link below:

https://www.subscribepage.com/speech-therapy-for-kids

Yasmin Akhtar

Introduction

I am the kind of person who is fascinated by language. The only job in the world for me was always going to be a speech and language therapist. As the years have gone by, I've felt there was a need to learn more with regard to different people's perspectives. I have spoken to hundreds, if not thousands of parents to see things from their point of view but more recently, I thought I would take things to a larger scale. That's when I sat down and had a cup of tea and a fascinating conversation with an English teacher.

She began by explaining why the English language was a complex one. The history of the small island and its numerous invasions has led to massive influences on the original language. We have had the Romans, Vikings, Germans and French, each leaving a significant mark on the language. Then she introduced me to this poem by Gerard Nolst Trenité, perfectly named 'The Chaos':

> *I take it you already know*
>
> *Of tough and bough and cough and dough?*

Others may stumble, but not you

On hiccough, thorough, slough, and through?

Well done! And now you wish, perhaps

To learn of less familiar traps?

Beware of heard, a dreadful word

That looks like beard and sounds like bird.
And dead; it's said like bed, not bead;

For goodness sake, don't call it deed!

Watch out for meat and great and threat,

(they rhyme with suite and straight and debt)

A moth is not a moth in mother.

Nor both in bother, broth in brother.

And here is not a match for there.

And dear and fear for bear and pear.

And then there's dose and rose and lose –

Just look them up – and goose and choose.

And cork and work and card and ward,

And font and front and word and sword.

And do and go, then thwart and cart.

Come, come, I've hardly made a start.

A dreadful language? Why, man alive,

I'd learned to talk it when I was five,

And yet to write it, the more I tried,

I hadn't learned it at fifty-five!

If you stumbled on a few of these chaotic examples, it's no wonder that children need some assistance learning the English language. Teachers and educators are well aware of just how challenging this experience can be and strategies are in place so that young children are able to grasp concepts early on. But every now and then, a child needs more than the support of parents and teachers. And this is where speech and language therapy plays a crucial role.

As a speech and language therapist, I have dedicated my career to helping children from all walks of life and with various speech and language delays and disorders, some mild and others complex. Another side of my job is to provide support for parents and carers. Over the years, I have witnessed how important it is for families to work together in order to help children master their communication skills. As a mum, I am blessed to be able to see things from both a parent's point of view and a therapist's.

Most of us who follow a career helping others often get frustrated that we can't help more people. For this reason, I wanted to share my expertise and experience with as many parents and caregivers as possible and the best way to do this is in a series of books dedicated to parents who need a little help. You have probably read enough heavy scientific research, so my aim is to present the information in a meaningful and practical way. Knowing full well how busy you are, I am also going to 8bv zzwe enjoy the process.

Every specialist will tell you that early intervention is the best thing for childhood developmental delays and conditions, but sadly, due to COVID-19, getting the right diagnosis and support may take a

Yasmin Akhtar

frustratingly long time. There is no way around this as you will need a diagnosis from a professional. Every child is different and there isn't a book or website in the world that can confirm a diagnosis. What we can do is confirm suspicions and provide you with tips, strategies and most importantly, games that you can start from home while you wait for a diagnosis.

We are going to look at some of the most common disorders that affect children's speech, language and communication skills, as well as therapies that can help. Certain therapies are more suited to different conditions and talking to your specialist team will help you to learn more about the best therapies for your child. That being said, you certainly won't do any harm if you want to start introducing your child to some of the ideas in this book. I would recommend that you take notes on what you try and the changes you have seen, so that you can discuss these with your speech and language therapist – either with your current one, or whenever you are assigned one.

Without further ado, let's get straight into just how amazing and complex child development is and those early milestones to look for and celebrate.

Part 1: The Diagnosis

Due to the stress and worry that parents are often under, I wanted to create a bite-sized book that had just the right amount of information to reassure as many parents as possible. In Part 1, we are going to become familiar with all of the terminology. If you have had meetings with specialists, you will know the terminology can be very overwhelming. We will also learn about the types of speech and language delays and disorders and when you should be concerned based on various important milestones. Once we have gained a better understanding of speech and language, we can move onto the therapies in Part 2.

Chapter 1:
Let's Start at the Beginning

No, we aren't going to go as far back as the birds and the bees, but it's great to go as far back as those early days of pregnancy and to look at some of the amazing milestones that children achieve in their early years. Speech and language development will often mean that not all milestones are reached by any specific age, particularly if there are other conditions involved too. The reason it is good to know about the early developmental stages is that the sooner a delay, disorder or condition is diagnosed, the sooner a treatment plan can be created.

Pregnancy

Ah, pregnancy! It truly is such a miraculous time in a woman's life. The sense of achievement when making an IKEA table is great, but no words can describe the sense of achievement when making a human being! I feel sorry for men as they will never be able to enjoy this experience. At the same time, they are so lucky because they will never experience the weight of pregnancy. Yes, there is the weight on your stomach, your thighs and your ankles! But I am talking about the weight on your shoulders. There is so much pressure on pregnant women, constantly worrying if they are doing the right thing or if there is something they could do better. Am I too young? Am I too old? Is this cup of coffee going to harm my baby? Then there is that all-time question: what if there is something wrong with my baby?

Many speech and language disorders have unknown causes. Some have ties to genes because of the increased chance due to family history. Some have been linked to environmental factors and some to cognitive. The point here is not to scare you. Even if you covered yourself in bubble wrap in a sterile environment, there are risks. This goes back to the amazing miracle of creating a tiny human being. Every minute during pregnancy, the foetal brain produces around 250,000 neurons. Sometimes, the neural pathways (imagine them as wires) get confused and will affect speech, language and/or hearing.

Yasmin Akhtar

Birth

Another thing that I think it is safe to say all women have in common is the fear of giving birth. Sorry, men, it's not that we don't think you aren't scared but you don't get to compare the difference here! There is the overwhelming fear that something is going to go wrong, that we won't be able to cope, our birthing plan will go wrong – and the pain! Again, before you start to panic, Johns Hopkins estimates that 8% of pregnancies have complications. Most of us are lucky to have access to highly capable medical professionals who are ready for the unexpected.

The other thing that you have to remember is that complications during childbirth are somewhat out of your control. It's not like because you didn't pay enough attention during the breathing prenatal classes, it's all your fault that there are now perinatal complications. This information isn't to look at how things could have gone differently. I have given birth and I can safely say that there wasn't a logical part of my brain that I could have controlled during those final moments. That being said, this wouldn't be the best book it could be if I didn't share the good, the bad and the informative.

There have been studies on the link between birth injury and speech/language delays and disorders. Asphyxia, a lack of oxygen during birth, can cause a form of brain damage called hypoxic-ischemic encephalopathy. Brain bleeds, infection, meningitis and mismanaged jaundice can also be linked to brain injury, and possibly to speech and language disorders.

Early Milestones

'The baby smiled for the first time!' No, Mum, that was wind, and certainly not the first! The early milestones are not intended to be a way to measure developmental progress, but they certainly have become key identifiers for certain health conditions. The difference is that a cold is easy to spot, thanks to the runny nose and horrible cough. There is no need to worry if some of these milestones aren't reached by the exact age, but it is something that you should bring up during checkups. Most of the early milestones are related to communication. However, I have added a few other special moments.

2 Months Old

Around this age, babies will flash their first smile and for many, this is our first big milestone. Babies will also be able to support their own head during tummy time. When they move their arms and legs, you will probably notice that the movements aren't quite as jerky as they were as a newborn. In terms of sounds, you might hear some coos and gurgling. They will also turn their heads towards a sound and in particular, try to look at their parents and start to recognise people a little further away. Around this age, babies might show signs of boredom but they also might be learning how to calm themselves by sucking on their hand, for example.

When to speak to your doctor:

- There is no reaction to loud sounds.

- They don't smile at people.

- They can't hold their head up during tummy time.

- They don't follow objects as they move.

4 Months Old

The smiles will be more apparent, especially with those people who they recognise. They might also be able to copy you when you smile or frown. They will be able to follow an object with their eyes and the hand-eye coordination begins to develop, like reaching out for a toy. This age is a bit of a relief for parents as babies are able to hold their heads up without support and you might see them pushing themselves up onto their elbows during tummy time. They should be able to bring their hands to their mouth and if you hold them up so that their feet are on a hard surface, they should be able to push down on their legs. This is often part of their checkups. Emotional development is quite significant. They can tell you if they are happy or sad and you will start to hear different cries for tiredness, hunger etc.

When to speak to your doctor:

- They can't move one or both of their eyes in all directions or they don't follow objects with their eyes.

- They aren't making any sounds.

- They don't smile or bring objects up to their mouth.

- Their head isn't held steady.

6 Months Old

Things start to get more interesting now as babies learn how to roll over. There could be some shuffling around, more often than not going backwards before forwards. The urge to move is often brought on by the urge to try and get things that are out of their reach. Once holding a toy, they can move it from one hand to the other. This is the age that babies like to bounce on their legs when you support them standing up. They will also get better at sitting without support. Playtime becomes more interesting and you might start to hear special sounds when they are having fun. Babbling is more frequent and the first stages of a conversation are beginning, albeit not with words. Many six-month-olds start to respond to parents with stringed vowel sounds such as /ah/ and /oh/ followed by some consonant sounds, often /m/ and /b/. They should respond when you say their name.

When to speak to a doctor:

- They can't roll over or try to get things that are out of reach.

- They don't laugh or make sounds of enjoyment, like little squeals.

- They don't show signs of affection with people they are comfortable with.

- There are no vowel sounds.

- Their body appears too stiff or too floppy.

9 Months Old

If you have been trying to work from home with a nine-month-old, you will have learnt that your laptop makes a perfect hiding place for peek-a-boo, and that pen you keep trying to hide – they will be looking for that too. They will be learning the art of pinching things between their thumb and index fingers and now confidently put things in their mouth – one of the more dangerous milestones! Babies at this age can often get themselves into a sitting position and might start to pull themselves up to standing, or be able to stand while holding onto something. Crawling likely begins at around this age. They can point to things with their fingers, especially their favourite toys. More sounds are being made and they will understand the word 'no'. It's normal for babies to start getting a bit clingy with their parents and to also be afraid of people they don't know.

When to speak to a doctor:

- They can't sit with support or bear weight on their legs with support.

- There is no babbling or they don't respond to their name.

- They can't move objects from one hand to another.

- They don't recognise people who they know well.

- They don't interact with back-and-forth games (e.g. rolling a ball to you and you roll it back).

1 Year Old

The great milestone is that all-important birthday! 365 days and you couldn't imagine your life any other way. As your little one pulls themselves up, you might notice they start to take some steps while holding on to furniture, and they might be able to stand alone or take a few steps. Curiosity is strong and they like to play with different toys and, in particular, make lots of noise. They might also enjoy exploring by putting things inside containers and taking them out again. Some words will be clearer, like 'Muma' or 'Dada', and they might try to say other words. They will probably start to copy some of your gestures, like shaking their head to say 'No'. Communication is improved by the help of changes in their tone. They will also understand simple instructions and requests. It's possible that they will start to hand you a certain book. Some children at this age can start to drink from a cup or attempt to use a hair/toothbrush.

When to speak to a doctor:

- They develop a certain skill and then lose it.

- They aren't saying any single words.

- They aren't crawling or standing with support.

- They aren't pointing to things.

- They haven't learnt any gestures such as waving or head shaking.

18 Months Old

There are some significant emotional and social changes at this age. You may have already noticed that your little one gets upset when a parent leaves, or that they are much closer to you in social situations. It's too soon to understand the social impact of COVID-19 on toddlers and young children, but lengthy lockdowns might have played a role in your child's confidence in social situations, so that they will stay all that much closer to you. And you may also notice them warming up for these tantrums. They might be stringing various words together, and don't be surprised if one of those words is 'no'. Their vocabulary will be expanding at an incredible rate and they will know the words for many everyday objects. They can probably hold a pencil or crayon and scribble, and pretend play begins to develop. They should be well on their way to walking alone and possibly a little bit of running. Drinking with a cup will be less messy. However, seeing them start to feed themselves with a spoon can be entertaining!

When to speak to a doctor:

- Again, they develop a skill and then lose it.

- They are not walking.

- They are unable to copy other people.

- They aren't learning new words and they don't know at least six words.

- They don't react when a parent or carer leaves.

- They don't point to things to show you.

2 Years Old

This is the age when little people start to test their boundaries. It's that moment that they look at you when you say 'No' but continue what they are doing to see how far they can go. At the same time, they are starting to become more independent and you might see them happily playing by themselves for short periods of time. It's also around this age that your little one will start to become more interested in playing with other children. With regards to speech development, they can now form short sentences, up to around four words, or at least should be putting two words together to ask for what they want, e.g. 'More juice'. They will also be able to follow two-step instructions such as 'Take your shoes off and put them away.' When you are reading with them, they will probably enjoy pointing to images and naming some. If they haven't yet, they may begin to run, kick a ball, and more worryingly, begin to climb on furniture.

When to speak to a doctor:

- They can't use everyday objects (or pretend play) – for example, a spoon or a telephone.

- They are walking but rather unsteadily.

- They aren't linking two words together.

- They don't copy actions and words.

Is the Milestone Essential for a Diagnosis?

Medical practitioners need milestones as an age to use as a median. You too can use the milestones as a guideline but if you are concerned before, you can still talk to a doctor as extensive research has proven that early intervention is ideal.

The Centres for Disease Control and Prevention (CDC) also states that early intervention is best. Naturally, there are a number of other milestones in the early stages of development but as the diagnosis is usually between 18 and 24 months, it's these first achievements that are most relevant to your child and getting the right diagnosis. At a two-year checkup, you will be able to voice any worries you have. Nevertheless, if you have any concerns beforehand, it is definitely worth consulting a medical professional.

If you have ever run a marathon (and no I haven't, so I will use my imagination, like many of you), you probably did not set out with the intention of coming first. You could have expected to come in 10th, 100th or 1000th. The point is that you reached your goal and you celebrated. Try not to get bogged down by the pressure for little people to achieve their milestones. I have been there! The only thing you do when comparing your child to others creates stress, which your child will pick up on. Every milestone is a momentous occasion for the whole family and should be celebrated. Remember that celebrating isn't the same as spoiling. Your 20-month-old may have just taken their first step, but there's no need to rush out and get them a tablet.

Let's assume that if you are reading this book, it is because you do have concerns about these early milestones. This doesn't mean that you need to have ticked all of them, but there might be some things that are niggling at you. In the next chapter, we are going to look more specifically at speech and language development.

Chapter 2:
Speech and Language Development

While our first chapter looked at child development in general, we are now going to focus more on speech and language development and some of the issues that may arise. Many children won't fully communicate until they are around five years old, but it's from birth to three that is most crucial for a child's speech and language development. This is a time of intense maturity of the brain and in particular, the ability to develop speech and language skills. We have heard of toddlers' brains being compared to sponges and this is very much true. The more you can expose your little one to language at this age, the easier it becomes for them. Still, there are some children with speech or language disorders who won't reach these important milestones, regardless of how much language they are exposed to.

Speech and language disorders tend to be grouped together but there is a difference. When we talk about a language disorder, we refer to problems that children have in understanding what people are saying, or in expressing how they feel. On the other hand, children who have difficulties with sounds, syllables, forming words or a stutter will have a speech sound disorder.

There has also been much debate on the two terms 'developmental language disorder' (DLD) and 'specific language impairment' (SLI). It's true that many people, professional and non-professional will use them interchangeably and a lot of the research you may have found doesn't specify a clear difference. We are going to stick to the term DLD as many would agree that SLI is very specific and it is more likely that a child's issues with speech and language are related to other conditions, rather than just one. In the UK, the term 'speech, language, and communication needs' (SLCN) is widely used.

Bilingual Speech

As globalization encourages more immigration and migration, it is more common for children to be brought up in bilingual environments. It leads to the ambivalent question of whether children with speech and language disorders should be introduced to a second language.

When should you introduce your child to more than one language? And should you even attempt to, if you have identified a DLD? Here is where things start to get a little trickier but nothing is impossible! It is worth bearing in mind that speech and language research is still relatively young and the same can be said for bilingualism. So far, we know that bilingual children can gain higher educational achievements, improved use of language in social situations and better cognitive flexibility. There is not enough research to indicate the long-term effects of children learning two or more languages when also coping with speech and language delays or disorders.

Let's look at both sides of the argument. Some feel that if a child has difficulties with one language, it is going to be even harder to master a second. For this reason, parents are advised to speak their main language at home, or if they have more than one home language, then keep to the 'one parent, one language' rule, where each parent consistently speaks only one of the languages to the child. On the other hand, taking advantage of these early years, when the brain is such an absorbent sponge, exposes children to more vocabulary. At this age, they are also not concerned about the fact that they are learning two languages. It's not like us adults who have to translate and question every grammatical structure! They listen and learn. Of course, going back to the original point, children with speech and language difficulties aren't going to be able to listen and learn the same way other bilingual children do. Finally, the Multilingual: Empowering Individuals, Transforming Society project (MEITS) states that reducing the number of languages a child with speech and language disorders speaks isn't going to cure the disorder. Instead of a bilingual child with speech and language disorders, you have a monolingual child with speech and language disorders. Furthermore, a bilingual or multilingual child is likely to experience speech sound difficulties in all of the languages they speak if these languages share the same speech sounds. And often, this will be key to deciding the next steps.

One of the generally agreed arguments against encouraging bilingualism in conjunction with speech and language disorders is the available resources. Logically, UK therapists are trained in providing therapy in English; therefore, you will be offered therapy in English. Having said that, you are encouraged to use your home language when working on your child's targets at home, especially if your child is not yet in school. When your child is in nursery/school, the same strategies are sent to school for staff to work on with them to keep the support consistent at home and in school.

As a mother, with experience in both bilingualism and speech and language development, I can only offer you this advice. Weigh up all the pros and cons of your child's individual situation. Speak to your team of specialists and get as much insight from them as possible, based on the resources that are available. For example, if one of the play-based therapies is what your team is recommending for your two-year-old, it makes sense to practice the strategies in your mother tongue if that is the language you mostly speak at home. However, if your five-year-old is attending school and they have been given speech therapy work to develop their English language, then you should try and practice the therapy strategies in English, and you can practice the therapy at home. It makes sense that your sessions are in English but you should use your home language at home during play and interaction to continue developing the home language. No situation is going to be the same and there is no clear yes or no answer to this topic.

Receptive Language

Receptive language is the language that we take in and understand. You can see the development in various levels.

12-18 months: A child will be able to understand simple information-carrying single words or keywords. For example, if you ask your 15-month-old child to go get you the TV remote, they will be able to understand. You may initially need to use gestures to support their understanding, so you may point to the remote and say, 'Get **remote**.' Children at this age can understand some verbs that you use routinely in the home such as 'sleep', 'eat', 'drink'. The child will be able to point to their body parts when you name them. For example, 'eyes', 'nose', 'mouth'.

2-3 years: A child begins to understand instructions containing two information-carrying words. For example, 'Give **teddy** a **spoon**,' when there is an option of a dolly and teddy and an option between a spoon and a cup. Children will begin to understand the functions of everyday objects. For example, they will know that scissors are used for cutting, a hairbrush to brush your hair and a toothbrush to brush your teeth.

3-4 years: Children will understand instructions containing three information-carrying words. For example, 'Give **teddy** an **apple** and a **banana**.' Remember, for an instruction to count as a keyword, you have to have another option for the child to choose between, otherwise all they have to do is to pick up the one object which is there in front of them.

At this age, children should be able to understand the concepts of size, like 'big' and 'small'. Children should also be able to understand and name different colours.

4-5 years: At this age, children can understand instructions containing four information-carrying words. For example, 'Put the **spoon** in the **drawer** and **cup** in the **sink**.' This is when the child is in the kitchen, and they can see both the spoon and the cup and a couple of other items in front of them. Remember to have other options, otherwise it won't count as a keyword.

Expressive Language

Contrary to receptive language, expressive language is how we express ourselves. You have already been given the basic information in Chapter 1. Children between 12–18 months should have lots of single words/nouns/names of people/things. For example, 'mummy', 'daddy', 'cup', 'spoon', 'dog', 'house', 'chair', 'book' etc.

Yasmin Akhtar

When the child is two years old, they should have around 150 to 300 single words. I know you are thinking: that's a lot of words! I assure you, if you sit back one day and start taking notes, you will be surprised how your typically developing child is picking up the language.

However, I can understand the reason you may have bought this book could be because your child is not saying many words, if at all. We will discuss that a little later in this chapter.

When your child has a large single-word vocabulary, start adding language to their single words. You need to add another word to their single word and say two words back to them. Your little one should hopefully be able to have a mini-conversation with you using two-word phrases such as: 'More juice', 'Daddy car', 'Go out', 'My turn' etc.

The more you model the language by repeating (correcting without the child knowing you are correcting), the quicker they will learn. For example, if your child says, 'Chair,' you can say, 'Yes, this is

Daddy's chair.' If your child is pointing at you while you drive and says, 'Mummy car,' you can say, 'Yes, Mummy's driving the car.'

We will talk more about the strategies to develop understanding and talking in the therapies chapter.

We have looked at the language development of a typically developing child. Let's now look at some of the difficulties you may encounter. Your child may have delayed language – at two years old, your child may only have about 30 single words and they may not yet be putting words together to make two-word sentences. If there are no other health issues or concerns, then hopefully your child will continue to develop their language skills but will need more help from you.

Communication Before Words

Take a moment away from the kids for a minute and let's think about our communication without words. Think about a time when your friend had a mouthful but waved frantically at a napkin, or the shop assistant that gave you the warmest smile. What about the look of your favourite person, when you can just see their love for you in their eyes? Not all communication is about words. As parents (and I have been there), we get so caught up with the milestones and waiting for that all-important first word that our vision is cloudy and maybe our ears are a little blocked.

Communication starts far sooner than words. When a baby cries, they are telling you that something is wrong. When you go to them and they hear the sound of your voice, they are calmed. You could be saying 'There, there, my darling,' or 'Dear me, we still have to walk the dog and get the washing out.' It's your voice, not the words that have the calming effect.

What Are the Stages of Communication Before Words?

- **Pre-intentional:** This is where your child smiles, vocalises or babbles but there is no message behind this communication.

- **Anticipatory communication:** Your child starts to anticipate your reaction.

Think about a peek-a-boo game. You hide your face with your hands then move your hands and say 'Peek-a-boo'. If you do this often, your baby will begin to anticipate your action and look forward to it. They might show this by smiling or wriggling or moving their arms/hands, even before you say the words.

- **Intentional communication:** Your child moves their hands or body, makes a sound or does an action like tugging at your clothes or taking your hand and leading you somewhere – they intentionally want something to happen or to communicate their feelings/intentions.

- **Words and ideas:** Children develop words, and they will begin to use them to express their feelings, comments, questions and ideas.

- **Joining words and ideas:** The more words they acquire, the more they will start

> to put them together into sentences to express themselves.

We have talked about how babies use pre-intentional and anticipatory communication. However, it is important to remember that some children who are much older may be at a pre-intentional level due to their speech and language delay/disorder, related to complex medical issues. You will need to target your support towards developing their skills at their existing level of communication. Don't look at their age but their level of understanding. For example, if your child is five years old, they have complex needs and their communication level is anticipatory, so you need to work on the next level which is intentional communication, and not on words and ideas as that is a big jump. Despite your enthusiasm, you need to adjust your expectations.

The quality of your language skills is going to play its role. I have a family member who speaks so incredibly quickly, I can barely understand her. I have another who adds 'like' between every other word. My gran was very well-spoken. I know people who speak painfully slowly to babies and children or in such a high pitch that I think they have sucked the air out of a helium balloon. There is no need to become obsessed and start instructing family members as to the rules of communicating with your little one. However, you can gently remind them that there is no need to dumb it down, and that they ought to use the correct words for objects and use as much different vocabulary as possible.

Communication is a combination of both speaking and listening – or in your case, watching. Watch how babies react to different sounds, music and rhythms. Watch to see what they are pointing at and listen to those first babbling sounds that are made. When you speak, let them have a turn for their babbles, as this is communication in the real world – speaking and listening. As they get a little older, use words for the things that they point to. You don't need to have lots of expensive toys to boost early communication. Colours, textures and sounds are the key. Saucepans, wooden and plastic spoons, dishcloths and sponges, and odd socks filled with different materials are just

Yasmin Akhtar

some of the ways you can spark a baby's interest and start expanding vocabulary and communication before words.

There is plenty you can do to encourage a communication-rich environment prior to your little one's first words. A parent's favourite word is 'routine' and for great reasons. Establishing a good routine provides opportunities to repeat activities. Repeating activities leads to repeating vocabulary! We will talk more about this when we look at the therapies you can do at home.

Chapter 3:
Language Delays and Disorders

If you are reading this book, it could be because you have some suspicions about problems your child may have with communication. It might also be that you have received a diagnosis and are looking for more help. There is still a grey area in between. Because every child is different, to get the best strategies to help your child, you need a diagnosis. I discourage anyone from reading this book and then taking things into their own hands. I know I am repeating myself but that is how important this is!

It's a tough time for parents when they see their child is struggling in one way or another. The first place people often turn to is the Internet, but then with so many abbreviations, terms and medical lingo, they can feel more lost than when they began. We have plenty of time to get down to all the different therapies, so let's take a moment to go over some of the common terms that you will hear, so that you are more familiar with them and above all, can feel a little less intimidated by them.

Yasmin Akhtar

What Is the Difference Between a Delay and a Disorder?

The first question is whether your child has a delay or a disorder. As you can imagine, when we talk about a speech or language delay, it means that your child is making progress with their language development, but they might be doing so at a slower rate than their peers. They are reaching the important milestones but not by the usual age. On the other hand, a speech or language disorder is when a child isn't developing the appropriate skills or developing them in a manner that is considered atypical.

What Is the Difference Between Receptive and Expressive Language Disorders?

I like to view this as 'what goes in and what comes out', although as a therapist, I will put it more professionally. It is important to mention here that children learn to understand a language before they can speak it. Receptive language disorders are when children struggle to understand the meaning of what is being said to them. They may only understand the basic instructions but will struggle to understand more complex language, or they may not understand even the basic instructions. This can be in the sense that they can't comprehend the language, or that there are problems with their hearing.

Expressive language delay is where your child is not able to communicate with you using verbal or non-verbal language. Disorders of language are where the child's language skills are developing but not in a typical or normal pattern. These children will face challenges when they are not able to express their feelings or needs. Don't forget that around the age of two, toddlers experience a phase of becoming frustrated because they know what they want but don't have the skills to communicate. This is a normal stage of development but can become a concern if it doesn't pass.

It is also possible that children have difficulties with both receptive and expressive language. If you have ever been on holiday to a foreign country and tried ordering a meal in a different language, you can understand maybe a fraction of their frustration.

Yasmin Akhtar

Speech and language delays and disorders are sometimes related to other health issues. In many cases, children are bright and healthy and with help from a professional speech and language therapist, an effective plan can be put into place.

Developmental Language Disorder – DLD

DLD is more common than most realise, with approximately 1 in 15 children living with it. It is quite a general term for children who have trouble understanding and using language. It could be with creating the right sounds, using the right grammatical structures and/or with limited vocabulary. Younger children may find it hard to remember new words and as they get older, it is difficult for them to recognise that words can have different meanings, like the bark of a tree and the bark of a dog. Children with DLD might struggle to describe how they are feeling, telling stories and understanding longer sentences. Although intellectually they can be quite smart, their challenges with language can lead to difficulties with learning and socializing at school.

Again, the exact cause of DLD hasn't been discovered yet. It could be biological, cognitive, environmental or a combination. Diagnosis often does not happen until the school years, when parents and teachers are able to see the struggles a child is having. Because language is crucial for all subjects, you might notice generally bad grades and less progress than children in the same year group.

Raising awareness of DLD will help with early intervention and reduce the risk of children going undiagnosed. You can look for RADLD in the UK, a movement made up of parents, educators, researchers and health professionals to raise awareness of DLD.

Some general red flags include a poor understanding of language, poor use of gesture and a family history of language impairment. When looking at specific ages, DLD may present in the following way:

1–2 years old:

- Your child is not using babble.

Yasmin Akhtar

- They don't respond (with words) when you speak to them.

- They are not attempting to communicate with you.

2–3 years old:

- Your child still has no words or signs.

- They are still not really responding (with words) when you talk to them.

- They may have had words but now they are not using them any longer or they have stopped developing more language.

3–4 years old:

- At this age, your child is only using two-word phrases.

- They are still struggling to understand simple instructions.

- Your child's speech is unclear so that even close family struggle to understand them.

- Some of the other things you may notice: your child using jargon instead of words, echolalia, repeating adult speech rather than using spontaneous language or being slow to develop verbs.

4–5 years old:

- Their interaction will be inconsistent or abnormal, with poor understanding.

- At this age, your child might be using three-word phrases.

- Their speech will be a little clearer, and the family will be able to understand about 50%, but strangers will not be able to understand your child's speech.

5 years old:

- Your child may find it difficult to retell a story or describe what they did in school.

- They will find it difficult to understand what they have just read or listened to.

Yasmin Akhtar

- Your child may have trouble remembering what they have been asked to do (recalling instructions).

- Your child can talk a lot but they are not good at to-and-fro conversation.

- They may interpret the information heard quite literally – they may not get the point of the information given.

- Other things you may notice -they will use sentences, but the words will be in the wrong order.

One of the most effective therapies for this is to make things visual. You can encourage your child to use visual aids to get their message across, such as drawings or photographs. Also, try to use simple and repetitive language to make it easier for them to understand.

What About Dyslexia?

Despite dyslexia being a disorder that affects written language, it is still something that speech and language therapists can assist with. Those with dyslexia will have problems recognising words, letters and symbols. Reading will be hard and there might be difficulties pronouncing certain words. They will struggle with spelling and may write some letters or numbers back-to-front. A speech and language therapist can work with dyslexic children to improve their phonological awareness – specifically, things like rhyming, segmenting and blending syllables, identifying initial and final sounds of words and sound manipulation.

Aside from speech and language therapy, if your child is showing signs of dyslexia, you might want to speak to their school and ask for a referral to an education psychologist for an assessment. The education psychologist may then advise using coloured overlays for reading time. These are transparent films that can be placed over text to reduce the visual stress. It is important to speak to your child's school if they are not already aware of your child's struggles with reading and writing. The advice and resources provided by the education psychologist will have greater effects on the child and the progress they can make. I must also mention that schools have their budgets and they usually refer the children with the most severe difficulties. Therefore, please be prepared for school to say no if your child's difficulties are mild.

Chapter 4:

Speech Sound Delays and Disorders

Now that we have cleared up the difference between a delay and disorder, I am going to use 'disorder' universally just to make for easier reading. All of the typical speech and language disorders I discuss in detail now can be seen as a delay or a disorder, with the exception of those related to hearing. This list is in no way by order of severity. Early intervention is always the best plan of action, so if you are worried or something rings a bell, don't hesitate in contacting your healthcare provider.

Articulation Disorders

Articulation disorders are those where a child's speech sounds are developing but not in an expected pattern. The children will mispronounce sounds over a longer period of time than they should. One example is omitting sounds either at the beginning or at the end of words. For example, a child might say 'do' instead of 'dog' and 'bi' instead of 'bike'. On the other hand, additions are when a child adds an extra sound in a word. Instead of 'car' they might say 'cart' or 'buhlack' instead of 'black'. Additions are not as common as other articulation disorders. Some children will use substitutions: they will switch one sound for an incorrect sound. 'Very' could be pronounced as 'bery' and 'red' as 'wed'.

If a child needs support with sound distortions, it is because they have most of the words correct but there will be some distortion. The most common distorted sounds are /l/, /r/ and /s/. The /s/ sound can be produced from the side of the mouth rather than over the centre of the tongue. You may notice a whistling sound, so 'sheep' is pronounced more like 'shleep'.

Phonological Disorders

Articulation disorders are motor-based, whereas phonological disorders are neurologically based. Family members might be able to understand the child but others may not. Cluster reduction involves groups of clustered sounds, such as /sn/, which are mispronounced with the /s/ being dropped completely. 'Snap', 'snail', 'snake' would be said as 'nap', 'nail' and 'nake'. Another disorder is final consonant deletion. It is typical for children not to omit certain final consonants but all of them.

Velar fronting and stopping are related to sounds and the flow of air. If you say the words 'cat' and 'gold', you will notice that your tongue pushes up against the roof of your mouth, towards the back, and this stops air from flowing. This occurs with /k/ and /g/ sounds. Velar fronting means children can't position their tongue in such a way so these /k/ and /g/ sounds are pronounced as /d/ or /t/, which means that 'cat' would be pronounced as 'tat'. When we create fricative sounds, we need the flow of air for these long sounds, specifically /sh/. 'Sheep' has a long initial sound and without the air, children will replace the /sh/ with a short sound, perhaps saying 'tip' or 'pip'.

Apraxia

Inside our brains, we have special muscles. These muscles are what allow connections between our speech function and our brain. Apraxia is when these connections are lost or damaged, and despite knowing what they want to say, a person can't communicate it through words. So much so, they can effectively write what they want to say but without the link between the brain and the speech function, they can't verbally express it. Apraxia in adults is caused by brain damage but in children, the cause is unknown.

Apraxia can be very mild or can cause complete incoherence. Because the muscles, lips or tongue can't move in the right way, children may not be able to say much or they will have difficulties forming sounds and words. In mild cases, it can be hard to separate apraxia from other speech disorders. Some signs of apraxia in children include not saying words in the same way each time, or changes in sounds. They will often stress the wrong syllable in a word. You may also notice that shorter words are easier to pronounce but longer words aren't as clear.

Dyspraxia

Dyspraxia is a condition that affects planning and motor movements and is not limited to speech. To clarify the difference, we use the terms 'verbal dyspraxia' or 'dyspraxia of speech' because dyspraxia can also affect the limbs and/or the body. Some of the general symptoms of dyspraxia are messy eating or feeding difficulties, limited concentration, the inability to keep still or they may be clumsy.

Verbal dyspraxia can present as no babble in the early months; they will have little speech by the age of three and their progress with language will generally be slow. Like apraxia, it is a condition caused by weakness of the speech muscles and can vary from mild to severe. Dyspraxia can be acquired (through injury or illness) or developmental, presenting in children.

A child with verbal dyspraxia might find it difficult to put sounds in the correct order to form words – more so with longer, complex words. They might say a difficult word correctly but then not be able to repeat it well. Children can often take their time to find the word they wish to use. Another sign of verbal dyspraxia is a somewhat monotone voice because it is hard for them to correctly use stresses and rhythms.

Auditory Processing Disorder (APD)

This is a disorder that affects communication between the brain and the ears. After sounds enter the ear, there is some form of interference by the time the signals reach the brain, so the sound isn't heard normally. Children with APD can struggle to follow a conversation and recognise different sounds between similar words. The problem is worse when they are in a noisy environment, such as the classroom. This isn't the same as an autistic child who is overly sensitive to loud noises.

APD signs are not always easy to spot when other speech and language disorders are present. Diagnosis will be down to an audiologist and speech and language therapists, who can work with a child to help them through speech and sound therapy.

Hearing Loss

It goes without saying that a child who suffers from hearing loss is going to suffer from significant delays with speech and language development, and the earlier their hearing is lost, the more difficult it becomes. Hearing is essential for developing verbal language. As we know, children learn by observing and imitating adults in their environment. If your child cannot hear what you are saying, then they won't be able to copy your speech. It is important to get your child's hearing checked as soon as you notice they are not looking at you when you call their name, if they watch your mouth closely when you talk and of course if your child is over 12 months and is not vocalising. Some children get lots of ear infections, which can affect hearing, and these children are likely to have delayed speech sound development. However, once they have been assessed and received the required treatment, which will hopefully rectify any problems, the child should develop their speech in a normal pattern. However, they may still require help from a speech and language therapist.

Yasmin Akhtar

In the UK, children's hearing is checked at birth. If you have any concerns, please talk to your health visitor or your doctor; they will be able to refer your child to the audiology department who can assess and offer appropriate treatment such as grommets or hearing aids, depending on the severity of your child's hearing loss.

Speech sound errors are quite normal for young children. Some children will develop the correct pronunciations through hearing the adults in their environment or some one-to-one work with a parent, which is done through modelling and auditory bombardment, but we will talk more about this in the therapies chapter.

Other children will require professional help, as the errors they are making should be resolved by a certain age. For example, if your six-year-old child is still using a /t/ in place of a /k/ or your eight-year-old is still saying 'wion' instead of 'lion', then it is time to get some help from a speech therapist. It is quite normal for a three-year-old to say 'wabbit' or 'labbit' for 'rabbit', but not for a seven-year-old.

Speech Therapy for Kids

Children with hearing issues will have problems hearing and correctly producing the 'quiet sounds' such as /s/, /f /and /z/. These children will also reduce particular cluster sounds such as 'spoon' will be said as 'poon' and 'square' might be produced as 'quare'. Some errors are quite typical, and all children make those at some point while their speech sound system is developing.

Some children omit the sounds either at the beginning (initial sound of the word) or the end of the word. For example, you might hear your child say, 'be' for 'bed' or 'oft' for soft. You may also hear children delete a whole syllable at the beginning of a word – for example, 'banana' will be said as 'nana'. Again, this is normal at a young age, but if your six-year-old child is producing words like this then you need to seek professional help.

Assistive Listening Devices

An audiologist will decide if your child needs an assistive listening device. There are three types of assistive devices that help with hearing loss, or voice, speech and language disorders. Assistive listening devices (ALDs) will amplify sounds, particularly in environments with high background noise. Augmentative and alternative communication (AAC) devices help people to express themselves. AACs can be picture boards or they can be more technical, such as programs that convert text to speech. Finally, altering devices connect to devices like a telephone or doorbell, for which a light will flash to alert the user.

Glue ear is a common infection in children, especially those with Down syndrome. Glue ear is a build-up of fluids in the middle ear and as a recurring issue, can affect speech and language. Grommets are tiny plastic tubes that are inserted into the eardrum, allowing air to flow into the middle ear. A doctor may recommend this procedure for persistent glue ear or ear infections. Grommets are a short-term solution and will fall out by themselves between 6 and 18 months after being placed. This can be enough time for the tubes between the middle ear and eardrum to mature and function correctly on their own.

Chapter 5:
Conditions That Are Affected by Social Situations

It won't always be the case, but there will be certain conditions that are exacerbated in social situations. This can be quite challenging for parents because at home, speech and language don't seem to be as challenging. Your little one might be happy to talk to you and their siblings, but as soon auntie and uncle rock up, everything changes. There are two things I warn against here. The first is pushing your child into social interactions for them to overcome their condition. Saying things like, 'It's only Auntie,' or 'Go on, go and play with the other kids,' isn't going to help because it is not something they can control. Which leads onto my second point. Be careful not to assume that your child is just shy. This is why I have gone into detail about milestones, what to expect and when to speak to a professional.

Yasmin Akhtar

Muteness/ Selective Mutism

A mute child doesn't speak at all. Selective mutism is when a child doesn't speak in various situations. Parents have to be very careful with selective mutism because they can often feel frustrated that their child will talk in some situations and not others. It might feel like they are being difficult or not trying hard enough. Selective mutism isn't about choosing not to talk, it's about not being able to, which makes this a psychological problem stemming from shyness to extreme anxiety. The diagnosis comes from a team of specialists, including a speech and language therapist and an educational psychologist. A treatment plan could be created together as the child may also have a speech/language disorder that is contributing to selective mutism.

ASD – Autism Spectrum Disorder

Because the autism spectrum is so varied, communication issues can range from non-existent or hardly noticeable to complete withdrawal or mutism. ASD children might have trouble with speech and language development, tone of voice and non-verbal communication. Generally speaking, speech and language disorders with ASD children lead to difficulties with social interactions.

Language can be quite repetitive, with some ASD children developing a condition known as echolalia, when they repeat the exact word or phrase immediately after hearing it, or delayed echolalia, when they will repeat it later on. Vocabulary can be limited, except for subjects that they are particularly keen on and then, they will have an amazing range of vocabulary.

Speech and language therapy will help a large number of ASD children learn how to communicate. However, there are some children who may not master speech and language skills. In these cases, therapists will work with the child to develop other forms of communication like symbol systems, gestures or sign language. You can find a lot more information about ASD in my book 'Understanding Autism, Walk a Mile in Their Shoes'.

Yasmin Akhtar

Are ASD and DLD Related?

The two conditions do overlap but they also have very distinct differences. You won't see repetitive behaviour with DLD and unlike ASD, DLD doesn't normally present with other conditions. ASD requires a medical diagnosis but DLD is less likely to be diagnosed by a medical professional and more likely by an educational psychologist. That being said, they are both life-long conditions which bring challenges in social situations, with expressing thoughts and feelings, and in understanding speech and language.

Stuttering/ Stammering

Stuttering is a common speech disorder that is also known as stammering. It is likely that you have had a stuttering moment, normally when you are nervous, or a certain event may trigger a stutter. In these cases, it doesn't affect your daily life and is not considered a speech disorder. Speech and language therapists consider it a disorder when it negatively affects daily life or a person avoids certain activities in order to avoid stuttering. Stuttering can also be developmental or acquired from illness, injury or psychological and emotional trauma.

The cause of stammering is unknown. It might be genetic, as approximately two in three people who stammer have a family history of stammering. It might also be due to the complexities of speech development. It's a very difficult process for young minds and sometimes, the neural pathways are 'miswired' or not connected just yet. Around 66% of children will grow out of their stammer. As well as working on emotions that cause the stammer (fear or stress), a speech and language therapist will create a plan to help improve your child's communication skills.

One thing that is going to help so much here – for which you don't need any speech and language therapies – is love and confidence. Praise your little one, and shower them with hugs and kind words. Give them extra time to speak, and don't complete their sentences. Acknowledge their struggles with talking. Be supportive and make sure everyone in the

Yasmin Akhtar

family has an opportunity to speak during family activities, even the child with the stammer. The more you help them accept their way of talking, the better they will become. Having said that, some older children may require support from a stammering specialist speech therapist, who will help you and the school to understand, and will give strategies to support your child.

Chapter 6:
Down Syndrome

Down syndrome isn't a speech and language disorder because it is a condition on its own. That being said, I wanted to talk about it as children with Down syndrome can develop speech and language disorders as well as social communication difficulties. This is a very complex area because Down syndrome can vary greatly in severity and symptoms. It is crucial that you follow the support provided by your specialist team. That doesn't mean that you can't use the therapies provided in this book, but for the best results, your team will be able to come up with a structured plan based on the individual needs of your child.

Down syndrome is named after the English physician John Langdon Down. Although Down syndrome had been around for centuries, it was Down who published the first accurate description. Those with Down syndrome have an extra chromosome. Instead of 46 chromosomes in each cell, they have 47, with the 21st chromosome being duplicated. Down syndrome can cause physical and mental disabilities but thanks to advances in science and society's understanding of the condition, many adults can lead fulfilling lives. This is particularly helped by early intervention.

Speech and language concerns are more likely to be delays rather than disorders for children with Down syndrome. However, that's not to say some children won't have disorders too. Another general tendency is that children with Down syndrome have better receptive language skills than expressive ones. This is because they are able to understand but have difficulties with grammar and tenses.

Another factor to consider with Down syndrome and speech and language development is the impact of hearing issues that many children will suffer from. Children with Down syndrome have shorter and narrower ear canals compared with other children. This can lead to a higher number of ear infections and therefore reduced or complete hearing loss. The frequency of hearing loss will affect a child's ability to hear speech and language – an essential part of the developmental process.

There is also a link between children with Down syndrome and working memory. The condition means that there is an impairment in the phonological loop. This phonological loop is what helps us to remember sound patterns and relate words to their meanings. This impairment doesn't affect the visual short-term memory, which is why visual aids are especially useful.

Children with Down syndrome can struggle to produce speech sounds because the condition affects their facial structure, nerves and muscles. Three things that can make oral-motor function difficult are smaller oral cavities, larger tongues and a higher arched palate. You know me by now, so you know I'm not saying this is the same for all children with Down syndrome. Just like not all boys with Down syndrome have difficulties with the structure of their lips and larynx. These are just some of the common physical causes of speech and language delays and disorders.

Yasmin Akhtar

It has also been estimated that autism is 15% more prevalent in people with Down syndrome than the rest of the population. This can complicate matters, not necessarily with their speech and language but with developing social skills. This is another reason why speech and language therapists can significantly help children with Down syndrome.

How Can a Speech and Language Therapist Help?

Some will argue that speech and language therapy is the most important intervention for children with Down syndrome. For cognitive development, children need vocabulary. Acquired language is then used to support thinking, reasoning and remembering. Even though these cognitive processes aren't spoken aloud, they still require vocabulary and language.

With vocabulary and language, children are better able to control their behaviour. If you look at the 'terrible twos', many toddler outbursts are due to frustration because they can't communicate what they want. Speech and language therapists can help children with Down syndrome to communicate how they feel and what they want or need. This greatly helps with their behaviour, which in turn makes social interactions easier.

It will still be parents who are the main therapists for children with Down syndrome and speech and language delays, as it is the day-to-day family interactions that provide a rich language environment. A speech and language therapist will help parents to target four main areas of comprehension: vocabulary, grammar, signing and reading.

Early interaction will involve your speech and language therapist teaching you the best strategies to use at home. A lot of this will be play-based. They will also be able to help with visual aids such as flash cards. Many children with Down syndrome are taught sign language to help them with their communication in the early years while their spoken communication skills develop.

For children with hearing difficulties, an ear, nose and throat (ENT) specialist might prescribe a low dose of antibiotics, or recommend grommets or hearing aids.

So, now that we have taken a good look at all of the potential speech and language disorders, you are probably keen to start learning what can be done to help your little one get the best communication start as possible. The following chapters will go over the therapies available and which of these you can do at home.

Part 2: Therapies

I like to think that at this point, the 'heavy' side of the book is done. You may be fairly convinced of the diagnosis and have already made contact with your doctor, or you are further along the process and your child has begun therapy. Hopefully you will be feeling more reassured and positive about the plan going forward. Now, you can move onto the lighter side of speech and language disorders – the therapies. In Part 2, we will discover so many ways that you can help your child, many of which are based on everyday objects you already have and play.

Chapter 7:
Parent-Child Interaction

Parent-child interaction is also known as parent-child interaction therapy (PCI or PCIT) and was developed in the 1970s. Dr Sheila Eyberg developed PCI from three parenting practices or developmental problems. These were Bowly's attachment theory research, Baumrind's parenting practices research and Bandura's social learning theory. After 50 years of research, advances and positive results, PCI has now been adapted for a number of childhood conditions from trauma and abuse to ASD and hearing loss.

What Is PCI?

The goal of PCI therapy is to teach parents how to interact with their children so that they can achieve the desired behaviour. For speech and language development, we have already seen the importance of the parents' influence as the main caregivers. With this in mind, therapists will work with parents so that they can improve their emotional communication skills and positive interaction skills. Basically, this is

71

done in the form of live sessions. Some therapists will video parents and children interacting and then use the video to highlight learning opportunities. Others will watch parents interact with their children in a controlled environment (like their office) and guide them by using an earpiece. Since the COVID crisis, PCIT sessions have also successfully been carried out online.

The structure of a PCI session will vary from child to child. The length of each session will also vary, but it is common to have one session a week. During this session, you will be given homework tasks and five-minute activities to work on throughout the week. There are two main focuses of PCI: child-directed interaction (which works on improving the relationship) and parent-directed interaction (when the focus is the behaviour).

There is no doubt that PCI has been revolutionary in the world of child development. Nevertheless, evidence to prove the effectiveness of speech and language development is still in the early stages. The most significant study was carried out on a group of

18 children with delayed language development and their parents. The results were extremely positive, seeing increases in utterances and repetitive vocabulary.

Let's take a closer look at the PCI process and in particular with one of the latest techniques, the VERVE child interaction technique. Keena Cummins has taken PCI and other related strategies to create an 'adult silent, child face-watching' technique that relies on videos for observation and self-reflection. The great thing about VERVE is that Keena Cummins is a speech and language therapist, so the technique concentrates on communication rather than behavioural issues children have.

There are five key aspects to VERVE:

Video: Parents are recorded interacting with their child. Each session is one hour long and there is a minimum of four 3-minute sessions, each building on from the previous session.

Endorse: Parents take one necessary interaction skill and work on that one in particular. The interaction skills could be naming, repeating, pausing, waiting for eye contact etc. When only one skill is the focus, there is less confusion and the child is better able to master this skill. Once this skill is mastered, the focus can be on adding another.

Respect: It is important that parents watch their videos so that they can share their thoughts, feelings and insights regarding their child's development. Parents need to feel valued and respected so that they can contribute to ideas that will help their specific family situation. Watching the videos is a great way to see their own interaction style and learn how they can make their own communication skills even better. The videos also offer an opportunity for parents to take a step back and see how much progress their little one is making.

Vitalise: The parents and the child are able to share in this vitalising experience. The parent gets to see how their skills are improving and the child gains more confidence in exploring and experimenting. Negative behaviours are reduced and replaced with positive experiences.

Eye contact: Parents wait for the child to engage in eye contact before speaking. This way, the child can hear the words and connect this to reading the parents' lips and facial expressions, all of which will improve language skills.

Who Can PCI Help?

Remember that parent-child interaction therapy can help parents with so many different issues, especially those related to behavioural problems. PCI can also be used for lots of different speech and language disorders but in particular, delayed speech, ASD, delayed social skills and hearing loss.

Delayed speech: Parents learn techniques to improve communication and not just in the therapy session. The parent can take the techniques learnt and they can be used throughout all stages of the child's development. For children with delayed speech, asking questions can cause them to feel quite anxious and this can add to their difficulty understanding. PCI focuses on commenting on the child's play. Commenting and repeating actions in play encourages engagement. Parents then learn to add words to the child's play to expand their vocabulary and grammatical structures to complete sentences.

ASD: What is extremely interesting about PCI and ASD is that studies have shown that after practising PCI, parents start to view their ASD child's problems differently, as if they are not as challenging as before therapy. ASD children that have social difficulties and speech and language disorders will often experience behavioural problems at some point in their childhood because of their frustrations. PCI can reduce behavioural problems and meltdowns by approximately 85% with children between 29 and 96 months. This type of therapy can also lead to an increase in self-esteem, which can enhance speech and language development.

Delayed social skills: PCI originates from Bandura's social learning theory. It makes sense, then, that this type of therapy can help children who have delayed social skills. The theory is based on the need for 'observing, modelling and imitating the behaviours, attitudes and emotional reactions' of other people. It's not that parents actively set the wrong social examples. We too have had to learn from the behaviours of others. PCI allows parents to correct potential problems with their own behaviour so that children have better role models in social situations.

Hearing loss: PCI can help parents to become more sensitive to their child's situation, teaching them how to be more responsive and emotionally available. One study followed 18 children between the age of two and six years old. They had 16 weekly sessions. Those children who received PCI therapy showed improved behaviour, social skills and significant improvements in their language skills.

PCI, PCIT and VERVE all sound rather basic but produce outstanding results. It's about taking the focus off the parent and allowing the child to lead play activities. The focus is on reinforcing positive behaviours so that the negative behaviours gradually disappear. It is a safe environment for the children, while providing massive learning opportunities for parents. Studies have so far been very small but the results are always favourable. The skills parents learn in PCI offer a new perspective for lifelong results.

Chapter 8:
Sign Language and Makaton for Speech and Language Development

Before diving into the differences between sign language and Makaton, we should lay a common myth to rest. Many parents are worried that learning sign language and Makaton will delay speech and language. Their concern is that a child will become comfortable using signs and this will discourage them from learning to speak. The latest research proves that the opposite is actually the case.

Research has shown that teaching children alternative communication doesn't prevent children from speaking but can support their ability to speak, whether the child is older or younger. Furthermore, it has also been shown to improve cognition in children who don't have hearing loss or learning difficulties. Imagine if you start signing with your baby; you are giving them a communication tool to use before the typical age of speech development. For children with speech and language delays and disorders, alternative communication enables them to communicate and this can motivate them to begin spoken communication because of the positive experiences they have had with signs.

What Is Sign Language?

The more specific question is, what is British Sign Language (BSL)? BSL is actually an official language that has been around for more than 250 years, ever since Thomas Braidwood founded the first deaf school in Scotland. In 2003, it was declared an official language, and just like British English, it has its own grammatical structure and even regional dialects. British Sign Language is used by children and adults with hearing impairments. For children who are born with hearing impairments, their first language will always be BSL. They might be able to learn spoken English with the help of assistive listening devices, which, if you think about it, is pretty cool because they will be bilingual.

Yasmin Akhtar

It's worth noting that just as American and British English have their differences, so do American and British Sign Language. Even from city to city, you will notice slight variations and colloquialisms.

BSL is made up of a combination of signs and fingerspelling. For example, you can sign the word 'sorry' by placing your right fist in the centre of your chest and making a circle in a clockwise direction. To spell words, you can create different forms with your fingers. Some of them are easier because they look like letters. For example, crossing your two index fingers is the letter 'x'. Even the not-so-easy ones have some relation. An 's' is made by hooking your right baby finger over your left baby finger. You can use your right index finger to point to the tips of each finger on the left hand (beginning with the thumb) for each of the vowels. Remember that for left-handed BSL, the actions will be reversed. The british-sign.co.uk website has some great resources to help learn British Sign Language plus a rather amusing fingerspelling game.

What Is Makaton?

In the 1970s, three speech and language therapists created Makaton as a communication system made up of signs and symbols. They were called Margret Walker, Katherine Johnston and Tony Cornforth and this is significant because if you take the first two/three letters from their first names, you have the word 'Makaton'.

Some of the signs are borrowed from BSL but the systems aren't interchangeable. The main difference between Makaton and BSL is that Makaton is used alongside speech, so it is a support for hearing children who require language development. Once their language has developed sufficiently, they will no longer use the signs and symbols.

Makaton uses both signs and symbols along with spoken words. For example, the sign for 'where' is both hands with open palms facing upwards and moving the hands in an outwards circle. The symbol for 'where' is a question mark. With symbols, it's important that the right symbol is used to ensure as much clarity as possible, so there can be more than one symbol for a word. A triangle is the symbol for the verb 'can', whereas 'a can of drink' is used when speaking of the noun. There are also two signs for the verb 'eat', depending on whether you are eating with your fingers or with cutlery.

The great thing about Makaton is its presence on TV. You can look out for 'Something Special' on the BBC, where Mr Tumble helps to teach children Makaton signs and symbols. Another favourite is 'CBeebies Bedtime Stories'. And it's not just for the children. You will notice Makaton making an appearance in soap opera storylines in 'Emmerdale' and 'Eastenders'.

Makaton is now used in approximately 40 different countries. Like sign language, you need to make sure the resources you use are specific to the language your child needs support in. Your speech and language therapist will have plenty of resources for you and you can use the makaton.org site, especially if you are looking for support in other languages.

Does My Child Need BSL or Makaton?

Really, that is going to be down to your specialist team. Remember that BSL is the language of the deaf community in the UK, whereas Makaton is used to help those children who can hear with communication difficulties. Both can bring about amazing changes in a child's learning and confidence and there is certainly no harm in you and your child watching a bit of Mr Tumble and learning some communication skills.

Parents and Children Demonstrating Simple Makaton Signs You Can Learn

Let's face it, all books are more interesting with a few photos. We have taken 20 of the common and simple signs that you can start teaching your children. I would like to take the time to thank all those parents and children from different countries who have contributed to this part of the book. You are stars!!

Yasmin Akhtar

Mummy (Thank you
Mani, 5, UK)

Sleep

Goodbye (Thank
you Emily, 2, Spain)

Brother (Thank you
Sophia, 13, Spain)

Sister

Biscuit (Thank you
Muhammad, 3, UK)

Eat (Thank you Kyro, 5,
South Africa)

Cake

I

School

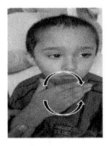

Teacher

Car (Thank you Aarvi, 3 Australia)

Sad

Listen (Thank you Elize, 3 and Mum, UK).

Drink (Thank you Indy, 10 UK)

Look

Daddy

Dinner

Chapter 9:
Therapies You Can Do at Home

This is quite a hefty chapter that I have filled with ideas. All of these therapies can be used for the delays and disorders that we have been through. You can either refer to a particular therapy your speech and language therapist has recommended, or choose what your child might enjoy the most. Don't feel like you have to go out and buy all of the latest toys and gadgets. There will be lots of suggestions for things you can use that are already in your environment.

All of these therapies can be used for both speech and language development. For speech, you can repeat the words they make mistakes within a clear way to encourage listening. For language, the sky's the limit. Use these therapies to expand on language structures like 'The toy is on the table/under the table/next to the table', sequencing like 'First we will... then we will' and of course, asking age-appropriate questions such as 'What do you want to do with the toy?'.

On that note, let's get started!

Helping Your Child Develop Pre-Verbal Communication

You really don't have to wait for their first words before you can start helping children grasp those early communication skills.

The 'Means, Reasons and Opportunities' model is based on the work by Dr Della Money in 1997:

Means: The means is the way in which a child communicates. As we have seen, this can be verbal like babbling and words and non-verbal, pointing, gestures, signs and symbols.

Reasons: A child's reasons for communication include expressing wants, needs and feelings. You will find that there are certain motivations that encourage the reasons. This can be things like their favourite toys, songs or games. Take some time to identify your child's means and reasons.

Opportunities: To encourage communication, you can now provide them with the most number of opportunities. To do this, you will often find that you need to take a step back. As parents, we get really good at anticipating our child's needs. We know they are hungry, thirsty or tired before they do. Because of this, we tend to prepare what they need before they ask for it. Our superpowers are backfiring because it means they don't have the opportunity to communicate. I know you will always want to help them too, but if you wait just a little bit, you will find that they start to approach you and tell you what they need or want. There are plenty of other ways you can set up opportunities. For example, give your child a piece of paper, but not a crayon – now there is an opportunity for your child to ask for crayons using their own means. You have the opportunity to add language to the actions, so you could say, 'Oh you want a crayon?' 'You want to colour with a crayon?' 'You want a red/yellow/green crayon?' etc. Give a yoghurt but not a spoon, give craft paper but no scissors, and so on. Put the child's favourite toy just out of reach or in a clear box, so that they will need your help to get the toy or the activity.

Objects of Reference:

- Objects of Reference' (OOR) is what we call the consistent use of objects as a way of communicating. An object of reference is any object which is used regularly to represent an item, activity, place, or person. Understanding real objects are the first stage of symbolic development.

- Objects can be used to represent activities, events, people or places.

- They can help people to understand and communicate about changes or daily routines. OOR benefits children who may have a visual impairment and or hearing impairment. Social communication or Autistic spectrum disorder (ASD) and or Learning difficulties.

- To introduce Objects of Reference, choose activities or events that the person does frequently.

- Find objects that represent that activity in a meaningful way to the child.

- Just before making a transition or doing an activity, show them the object and use simple language to tell them what is happening.

- Use the order in which the child develops their symbolic understanding and the stage of symbolic development your child is at: (real objects, miniature version of real objects, photos, line drawings, signs, writing)

- Things to bear in mind when choosing objects:

- Choose real-life objects such as car keys, which can be meaningful.

- Small versions of objects related to an activity may also be used but can sometimes be confusing for the child.

- Objects of Reference do not have to be a whole item but may have shared features, such as using a piece of a towel or cloth to represent having a bath.

- Consider the child's sensory needs – if they have a low tolerance for a particular texture it will not make a good object of reference.

- You may also want to consider if the item can be easily replaced if damaged or lost.

- Encourage your child to hold the object on their way to that activity, or until they see the person etc (bear in mind that it may take some time for the child to accept it).

- Consistency is the key! So use the same object, present it in the same way and use the same language to describe the event/person etc.

- Use the object to explain things to a child, so children may use objects of reference to make requests.

- Safety is also a consideration – the headphones are a good Object of Reference, but the lead could be dangerous. Also, consider can the item be cleaned easily if required? Can it break or cause injury, if they

Yasmin Akhtar

explore it with their mouth, is there a risk of swallowing or choking on the item?

- It may take time for a child to get used to OOR.

Strategies for Developmental Language Disorder (DLD)

- Get your child's attention and say their name before you talk to them or give instructions.

- Use visual cues such as gestures, photographs, drawings, acting things out.

- Use simple and Repetitive language.

- Give instruction in smaller chunks.

- Check for understanding. For example, after giving an instruction, ask your child, what does mummy want you to do? Repeat instruction if required. Give one instruction at a time. For example, go get you book. Go get your pencil. Sit down and complete your homework. Instead of saying, go get you book, pencil, and then sit at the table and complete your homework.

- Give extra time to your child to process what you have asked them to do.

- Give lots of positive praise.

- Ask/encourage your child to use non-verbal language to communicate and get their message across. Make communicating easier by accepting their non-verbal communication.

Selective Mutism – Strategies for school/outside of the home

- Accept non-verbal communication

- Reduce/remove pressure to talk

- Involve the child in the classroom activities where they don't need to talk. For example, ask them to give out books/pens/pencils/paper to their peers. Ask the child to help you collect things from the peers, however, don't just single them out as attention is not something this child will like.

- Include this child in the non-verbal adult led group activities.

- Give praise to all the children for good communication.

- If possible, have one key person who can spend 1:1 time with this child to build their confidence and rapport. With time the child may start to whisper and then hopefully talk, however please remember this is not where the child is being difficult it is because they genuinely cannot use their voice/talk, so being patient is the key.

Stuttering/Stammering Strategies:

- Balance questions with comments when interacting with the child.

- Ask yes/no questions where possible.

- Make sure the child who stutters has equal opportunities at home and in the classroom to talk just as their siblings/peers.

- Ask their siblings/peers not to talk for them.

- Do not complete the child's sentence if they start to struggle.

- Do not try and guess what they are trying to say....just give time, reassure that you are listening.

- Show your child you are listening – get down to their level and make eye contact.

- Give them extra time to finish speaking – do not interrupt.

- Slow down your speech rate – use lots of pauses when talking– this will help your child feel less rushed when they speak.

- Acknowledge your child's feelings about their stammer - Calmly say, 'I can see you are upset,' and reassure them that you are listening.

- If your child gives up on speaking, be open about the stammer, e.g. slowly say, 'I can see that word was hard to say'.

- Tell other people in your child's life about this advice so that everyone responds the same way.

Yasmin Akhtar

The Importance of Play and Social Communication

Now that we have looked at PCI, Lego therapy, and intensive interaction, you have probably started to appreciate the importance of play and not just for the children. Playtime can provide huge benefits to parents and other family members. We are going to look at two other play-based therapies, the first being Lego Therapy and the second is a series of Interaction therapies. Before looking at some amazing play ideas for different delays, disorders, ages, and stages.

Lego Therapy

A little fun fact for you: there are 62 pieces of Lego for every single person in the world!

I find that parents have a love/hate relationship with Lego. Tidying up all of those little bricks is a challenge and they just find their way to every impossible-to-reach place – under the sofa! It's also hard to find a parent who hasn't screamed after standing on a piece of Lego. On the other hand, once we sit down with our children and let our imaginations live a little, Lego is actually quite relaxing and takes away some of our built-up stress.

Playing with Lego has the same anxiety-reducing effect on children. It also teaches children how to overcome frustration, patience, creativity and concentration. And we haven't even begun to look at the advantages for speech and language development! Surprisingly, it took nearly 70 years for this incredibly popular toy to become used as a therapeutic tool, thanks to Dr LeGoff. The clinical neuropsychologist noticed how children with ASD and social communication difficulties were drawn to playing with Lego. When Lego play is structured, children can improve a number of social skills.

LeGoff's research found that young people between the ages of 6 and 16 made significant improvements in three areas of social competence after Lego therapy. These were in the initiation of social interactions with peers and the ability to maintain interactions, as well as the reduction of stereotypical behaviours. Two years later, LeGoff carried out another study that showed Lego therapy also helped to improve collaborative problem solving, task focus, sharing and taking turns.

How Does Lego Therapy Work?

Lego therapy is usually carried out with children between the ages of 5 and 17. The great thing is the level of difficulty can easily be adapted to any age group and for receptive and expressive language difficulties and social communication challenges. Normally, there are groups of three children and one adult. Each child plays one of the following roles – the Engineer (or Architect), the Supplier and the Builder. Let's take a closer look at each role:

The Engineer: The Engineer's job is to make sure the Supplier has the right bricks and that the Builder can get them all. They will explain how the Builder needs to make the model and answer any construction questions that may arise. Once the model is finished, they will check that it is correct.

The Supplier: The Supplier has to organise the different bricks that are needed. They need to listen to the instructions of the Engineer and hand the right bricks to the Builder. They can also ask questions if things need clarifying. The hardest part for the Supplier is to be patient in between turns.

The Builder: Once they have all the bricks from the Supplier and listen to the Engineer's instructions to put the model together, the Builder can ask the Engineer questions and again, they will have to learn how to wait between turns.

The adult in the group has to take a back seat and play the role of the facilitator and not the leader. If the adult takes over the role of either the Engineer, the Supplier or the Builder, there is a breakdown in communication among the group. The adult in the group is there to provide ideas and to intervene only when they feel like the group is becoming frustrated with the activity. To offer ideas, the adult can use things like a visual checklist or a naming guide for the Lego names. It is also important that the adult praises the children for all the steps that they successfully complete.

Yasmin Akhtar

What Can Children Gain from Lego Therapy?

Personally, I love the fact that children are playing with a toy that is unisex, non-discriminating and fun for all. Any play-based environment is going to help take away the anxiety that can arise from meeting new people and for older children, it can help to take away the stigma associated with traditional types of therapy.

Lego therapy can help children to develop motor skills and memory skills. It enables them to focus on sequencing and planning, all the while listening and asking for clarification. Children have to focus on visual images in order to create a tangible object, so aside from visual perception, there is a massive boost in confidence once the team has completed their task. This encouragement can lead children to want to try new experiences in other social situations. As for their language skills, they get to enhance their language concepts as well as their descriptive and positional language.

Who Can Lego Therapy Help?

Lego therapy can help any child who is struggling with speech and language development. The Engineer/Builder/ Supplier roles reinforce essential vocabulary and language structures that can be transferred to other areas of learning and life. For example, positional language helps children to understand things like 'on top of', 'next to' and 'beside'. Descriptive language increases their range of adjectives and adverbs. Depending on the age, they can also practise sequential concepts such as 'first' and 'next'. If you can imagine all of the things you can build with Lego, you can understand the possibilities of language learning.

More specifically, Lego therapy is the perfect tool for children who have speech and language difficulties due to social interactions. This could be selective mutism, stuttering, anxiety or of course autism. Taking children out of a busy classroom and working in small groups removes an awful amount of pressure from the child. They are able to feel safe and as the activity is child-led rather than adult-led, they may also have more confidence when practising their skills and trying to communicate. Over time, as a child's confidence begins to grow, they will be able to transfer the wide range of skills learnt through Lego therapy to other environments, like the playground or even small group activities within the classroom.

The better question might be: who is Lego therapy not suitable for? It is unlikely that you will see the full benefits of Lego therapy with children who have behavioural issues that don't stem from speech and language disorders. It may not be the best for children who have ADHD (attention deficit hyperactivity disorder). The problem here is that children with this kind of problem may end up disrupting the session or dominating a certain role. Imagine inviting two of your best friends for dinner along with the Queen of England – one is going to steal the show, whether she is aiming to or not! As each of the three roles requires speaking, listening and taking turns, it is best to establish a group that is, to an extent, similar.

Another amazing thing about Lego therapy is the free resources available. My favourite site is probably twinkl.co.uk., on which you can search for 'building block therapy'. You can print adult guidance, positional language cards, key word cards, building brick cards and more, all for free. There are also tons of videos on YouTube that can help you to become more confident at being the facilitator before introducing Lego therapy to your child. You could have a weekly 'Lego party' and invite two of your child's friends to come and play, if you feel this is the right move, or you may have siblings who are keen to help.

Intensive Interaction

The name of this type of therapy does sound quite daunting but intensive interaction can be quite fun. Like PCI, intensive interaction is a therapy that focuses on educating communication partners to achieve better outcomes. Let's start at the beginning.

David Hewett was a principal of a special needs school near London. Back in the early 1980s, there certainly wasn't as much information on special needs education as there is today. There were no teaching tools for those who have severe communication difficulties. Hewett wanted to teach his pupils but soon learned that if he and his staff couldn't break down the initial barrier and get to know his students, learning would be ineffective. Research on early interactions of infancy, along with careful trial and error and closely watching how the students started to react, led the way to intensive interaction.

The approach focuses so much on those all-important early interactions that it was originally called 'augmented mothering'. It takes the complex interactions of babies and toddlers in their first two years of life and applies those same early interaction behaviours with children who have more serious speech, language and communication difficulties. Studies showed that there were positive effects on both adults and children, and so the name was changed to 'intensive interaction'.

How Does Intensive Interaction Work?

Some people are a little taken back at first. The communication partner (most likely you) has to alter behaviours that would otherwise not be considered normal. The irony is that the interaction between a parent and a baby is probably the most natural interaction there is. Think back to when your little one was just a baby; here are some of the fundamentals of this early communication:

- Learning how to use and understand eye contact

- Reading and using facial expressions

- Learning how to use and understand physical contact

- Learning how to use and understand non-verbal communication

Intensive interaction takes these concepts and expands on them, adding things like:

- Developing concentration and attention

- Taking turns with their behaviour and interactions

- Copying sequences of other people's activities

- Appreciating and sharing personal space

- Learning to control levels of excitement

Above all, intensive interaction is about taking a step back and learning how to enjoy spending time with your child. Through no fault of our own, time has a habit of getting the better of us. Newborn babies – as much as we love them – really don't do much, yet we have the ability to just sit and watch them in awe. We find it within us to enjoy being in the slow lane for a while. Intensive interaction reminds us that the fast lane is only for certain occasions and not to be lived in!

What Does Intensive Interaction Require from the Communication Partner?

There are plenty of skills that a speech and language therapist can teach you. However, before that, I think it's essential that you have the right mindset. During intensive interaction sessions, you have to be all in, leaving the stress of the outside world and turning all of your attention to your little one. You need to be ready to have fun. The intensive interaction approach can then become part of your daily routine. This can be during routine activities, quiet times or when your child shows signs of wanting to be social. You can also set aside quality time every day to interact with each other.

A major change will be with your tone of voice, your eye contact and other forms of body language. These changes will allow you to be less threatening – and please don't take that the wrong way. As a mother, I would never want to see my behaviours as threatening, but as a speech and language therapist, I know that standing up while talking to young children can appear dominating, as if you are towering over them. When you get down to their level by sitting on the floor with them, all of a sudden, they can feel more relaxed.

You will also learn how to read the very subtle signs that your child is communicating to you. You may notice that your child looks away when they need a rest from the activity, or they might have a certain behaviour that calms them down. One psychologist noticed that a child would rub the palm of their hand with their thumb. When the therapist started to rub their thumb into the child's palm, the child responded by rubbing the therapist's palm with their own thumb. This was the first step of their early interactions, which blossomed so much that in time, the child would sing along with the therapist.

As with PCI, it is the child who should take the lead in choosing activities, while the adult is there primarily to comment and respond. There is also a need for rhythm and repetition, so that you can maintain the child's attention and it becomes easier for them to know what will happen next.

Potential Results from Intensive Interaction Therapy

Various studies have been carried out on children of different age groups, all with positive results. Research has found that intensive interaction increases social engagement and/or initiation, and there is more smiling, eye contact and looking at people's faces. Some studies have shown that children are more tolerant of physical contact. There have also been improvements in vocalisation. While every child is going to respond differently, parents would agree that children are generally happier after intensive interaction.

Who Can Intensive Interaction Help?

David Hewett, along with colleague Melanie Nind, has stated that intensive interaction is most effective for children and adults with S/PMLD – severe or profound and multiple learning disabilities, in particular those who are pre- or non-verbal. This would certainly include those children who have severe autism or Down syndrome. It will depend on your team of specialists and your child's learning needs as to whether they feel intensive interaction will benefit your child.

One thing that you should bear in mind is that intensive interaction requires specialist training. Unlike Lego therapy, it's not something for which you can download resources and begin at home. However, while you are waiting to see your speech and language therapist, you can still try some of the basic ideas we have looked at, especially things like dedicating time every day to get on the floor with your child, allowing them to choose the play activity and you observe and follow.

What is Social Interaction

Remember that we are still talking about a spectrum of difficulties for children when it comes to social interactions. You may notice your child coming across as awkward in social situations or the anxiety might be so much that they can't speak in social situations. It is important to remember that having a speech and language disorder does not necessarily mean this is guaranteed. Not all children with speech and language difficulties are destined to struggle with social situations. On the other hand, your child may speak well for their age but still need to work on their social communication. This is known as 'pragmatics', which is when children aren't able to learn the social rules that we need to successfully communicate with friends, family, teachers, etc. Here are just some of what we would consider acceptable social communication rules:

- Using an appropriate level of language for different reasons such as to greet people, request things and inform

- Changing or adapting the level of language depending on who you are talking to and in different environments, knowing how much information to give a listener

- Respecting others taking turns in a conversation

- Introducing a topic and remaining on topic

- Using the appropriate body language, gestures, facial expressions and eye contact

Now, it's not like you are going to witness your two or three-year-old master the art of social communication. They will open their mouths and say things that make you wish the ground would swallow you up. Social communication is something that is learnt over many years and even then, not every adult can say they get it right every time, especially when we consider cultural differences.

A speech and language therapist can help children with social interaction, even when a speech and language disorder hasn't been diagnosed. A lot of emphasis will be on play-based therapies and ideas to follow that you can use at home.

What is Early Interaction?

We have touched on early interaction on and off. It relates to how you can play with newborns and babies to enhance those first vital steps of communication. Early interaction includes all of the sounds a baby can hear, the looks on people's faces and different touches. Hearing Mum and Dad's voice early on is going to help support speech acquisition, and this begins before babies are born – they are listening to everything that is going on in the outside world from the safety of the womb.

We have an advantage with newborns. We are so amazed by them that it's easy to want to just sit and watch them, despite the fact that they don't do a great deal. This is the perfect time to begin early interaction. Newborns can see approximately 20-30cms away, so make sure you are close enough for them to see your face and the different expressions you make. It won't be long before they are able to focus their eyes on other objects, at which point you can start showing them different toys and household objects, telling them all about them. It will also encourage them to start reaching out and trying to hold objects.

Babies need to be held, and they need to feel the love and warmth from your arms. This is necessary for them to be safe and to start building up their

Yasmin Akhtar

confidence and self-esteem. Don't worry about molly-coddling babies and teaching them independence. They have plenty of time to be by themselves while they are sleeping. They will only have short attention spans at this little age, so there is no need to overdo it at this stage.

When your little one is a few months old, they will start to enjoy listening to you singing and saying rhymes. As with all interactions with children, regardless of age, you need to be fully engaged and relaxed. Don't feel like you need to constantly be in the limelight. Your early interactions need to involve taking turns, even if just to admire their beautiful smile and little giggles.

Children with delayed early interaction skills struggle with sharing toys with their siblings or peers in nursery. Some children are extremely shy and struggle to speak in nursery and join in with play activities with their peers. Some children are not able to initiate interaction – for example, even though a four-year-old child really wants to, they may not be able to ask if they can join a play activity their peers are enjoying. They may stand at a distance and observe their peers playing but are not confident enough to join in. This is where adult support is required to help these children engage with their peers and develop confidence in communicating.

Sometimes verbal communication delay is the biggest barrier for children, behind which they can be isolated if the right support is not put in place. Your speech therapist will be able to advise you to practise the interaction strategies at home with your child where you would involve the siblings, cousins or friends' kids, and then also advise the nursery to put strategies into place to help your child become better at engaging with their peers and adults within their environment.

Ideas for You to Practise Play at Home

In this section, we are going to list some of the best books, toys and games to help with developing speech and language as well as early interaction and social interaction.

Yasmin Akhtar

Books

It is just marvellous how many extraordinary books are out there for children. Some of the all-time favourites to boost speech sounds, language and rhymes are:

- 'The Hungry Caterpillar'

- 'The Very Busy Spider'

- 'Brown Bear, Brown Bear, What Do You See?'

- The 'Chicka Chicka' set

- 'Go, Dog, Go'

- 'The Rainbow Fish'

- 'Goodnight Moon'

- 'Where the Wild Things Are'

- 'We're Going on a Bear Hunt'

- 'Spot the Dog'

Personally, I love all of the Julia Donaldson books, particularly the Songbirds set that has been created with Oxford Owl and which focus on phonetics. You can also keep your eyes out for any age-appropriate touch-and-feel books to encourage engagement. If you are looking for more help with social interactions, you can find or create your own social stories, which I discussed at length in my previous book, Understanding Autism, Potty Training and Personal Care, Help your child accomplish basic hygiene tasks: Getting a haircut, brushing teeth, washing hands, bathing and more! You can click the link to purchase the book if you are interested. http://mybook.to/UAPTpersonalcare

Toys

There are some toys that pretty much every child has – apart from a Lego set! This will often include dolls, figures and farm animal sets. These are perfect to use in role-playing. Role-play allows children to act out situations that perhaps make them nervous or uncomfortable. It can help them to prepare for upcoming events and of course, there is a rich range of vocabulary and language concepts that can be learnt. Shape sorters are good for attention and prepositions. Play-Doh, like Lego, has endless possibilities in terms of vocabulary. Whenever possible, try to buy gender-neutral toys. There is no need for boys to play with certain toys and girls with others.

Games for Taking Turns

There are a number of fun board games that will teach children the importance of taking turns. 'Candy Land', 'Hi Ho Cherry-O' and 'Let's Go Fishing' are all suitable for children aged three and up. To begin this social skill earlier, you might prefer to stay away from board games as they have small parts that could be dangerous. You can use everyday activities to show your child how to take turns. It can be something really simple like stirring cake batter, where you have a turn, then they have a turn. Or you can use stickers, where they choose one to stick on their drawing, followed by you.

Jenga is awesome for all ages in terms of safety but for skill, not so much. Nevertheless, older children will enjoy removing bricks and younger children can take turns to place bricks on top of each other.

Games to Practise Eye Contact

'Pass the Smile' is a lovely game that can be played with just two people but it is better in a group. Sit in a circle and choose a facial expression – a smile is the easiest but you could also pass the wink, for example. One person, with a neutral facial expression, looks at the next person and smiles. The next person then takes the smile, looks to the next person and passes it on. You can also play this game with a ball.

For two people, you can play the 'Mirror Match' game. Sit in front of each other (or stand) and one person is nominated as the mirror. They have to copy everything that the other person does. You can start off with simple actions like facial expressions, and move on to the arm and leg movements. Puppets also have a magical effect on children and captivate their attention. When puppets 'whisper in your ear', children look towards your face.

How to Develop Imaginative Play on a Budget

Wouldn't it be great to be able to afford all of the best books and toys for our kids!! Life often isn't like that, but that's not a problem here. Here are four ideas that you can play with your children with things that you already have in your cupboards.

- **Homemade bubbles:** 1 ½ cups of water, ½ cup of washing up liquid, 2 teaspoons of sugar. You can use a wire coat hanger to make the bubble wand.

- **Playdough:** 2 cups of flour, ¾ cup of salt, 4 teaspoons of cream of tartar, 2 cups of lukewarm water, 2 tablespoons of vegetable or coconut oil. Stir all of the ingredients in a saucepan over a low heat until it becomes a ball. Leave it to cool for a while, divide it into smaller balls and knead a little with food colouring. Keep it in Ziploc bags and it will last a few months.

- **Social stories:** If you can't find one to print off, you can make up your own stories. Take photos of your child or download images. You can even just fold paper, write and hand-draw images if you don't have a printer. Your child could colour in your drawings.

- **Puppets:** Who doesn't have a handful of odd socks that the washing machine seems to have eaten? Take all of those socks and draw different faces on them. You can cut out felt shapes to stick on, or pipe cleaners, or anything else that you may have left over in your crafts box. If your child is at the stage of putting things in their mouths, be careful to make sure nothing can be pulled off the puppets.

Vocabulary Building with Food

Note: This will also help the fussy eaters try a variety of foods.

Yasmin Akhtar

Get ready to have massive amounts of fun and a fair bit of cleaning up afterwards but messy food play is well worth it. Take a tray and fill it up with food. You can use things like milk, juice, tomato sauce, mashed-up banana, mousse, yoghurt, you name it. If you want to keep it less messy, try dry foods like cereals, flour, sugar, cold cooked pasta or rice. Hide small toys (no choking hazards) in the food and take turns to find the toys.

If you are using liquids, you can then use the liquid in the tray to make handprint pictures. You can use some of the dried food with PVC glue to make pictures and the cooked pasta shapes can be threaded onto string.

What matters is that you are dedicating time to spend with your child to have fun and play. They don't need expensive toys because the toys aren't the role model, you are! Taking time to play with your child every day is fundamental for their learning and their confidence.

Speech Sound Development Strategies

Aside from the time that you dedicate every day to playing with your little one, you can also use some of the following speech sound development strategies throughout the day. That's to say, you can take advantage of opportunities in daily life to work on specific sounds that your child struggles with.

One thing that I would advise at this stage is not to keep correcting your child when they make mistakes with sounds, or at least focus on how you are correcting them. Our goal is to build up their confidence as much as possible. For this reason, try to correct them by repeating the word clearly with the correct pronunciation rather than saying things like 'No, don't say it like that, say it like this.'

Auditory Bombardment

In 1983, Hodson and Paden developed the auditory bombardment therapy practice, which is most commonly used alongside games in a speech and language therapy session – for example, at the beginning and the end of the session. The child is repeatedly exposed to multiple examples of phonological targets. Imagine you are in the kitchen together; you could repeat all of the objects you can see that start with the targeted sound /s/: 'saucepan', 'spoon', 'sink', 'sausage' and so on. Remember that this is still a listening exercise, so you need to repeat the words and not expect your child to say them.

Interestingly, the use and benefits of auditory bombardment can be seen in studies of cross-linguistic phonological acquisition. English children tend to acquire the /v/ sound later on in their development because it is not a common sound in the English language. For French children, they acquire the sound earlier on because they are exposed to it more frequently.

It's worth mentioning that Hodson now uses the term 'focused auditory stimulation' because of the slightly aggressive interpretation of the word 'bombardment'.

Rhyme/Rhythm

The one thing that practically every culture has in common is the use of rhyme and rhythm, not just as a teaching tool but also as a way of passing down traditions. Rhyming and rhythmic structures make it easier for children and adults to repeat and remember words. There are also links between the ability to pick up language skills and music skills. Musicians find it easier to decipher and create specific sounds and sound patterns. This is why, when you add music to rhyme and rhythm, you can further enhance your child's development.

I am the first to admit that breaking into a song in the middle of the day is somewhat 'Disney-like' but here are some rhymes that you can use during the day which, when repeated, might encourage your little one to sing along.

> *(To the same tune as 'Happy Birthday to You')*
>
> *Good morning to you*
>
> *Good morning to you*

Yasmin Akhtar

Good morning dear child's name

Good morning to you

Clean up, clean up

Everybody let's clean up

Clean up, clean up

Come on everyone!

(To the same tune as 'Here We Go Round the Mulberry Bush')

This is the way we put on our shirt

Put on our shirt

Put on our shirt

This is the way we put on our shirt

So early in the morning

Of course, don't forget all of the traditional nursery rhymes that we learnt as a child. A study has shown that if a child knows at least eight nursery rhymes by the time they are four, they will be one of the best at reading and spelling in their class. It's true that this applies to atypical children – however, it does emphasize the importance of these timeless classics.

Use of rhyme and similar sounds is a strategy we use with younger children who are having difficulties producing some sounds, when they are not aware that they are making errors when they speak. For example, a four-year-old child is reducing cluster sounds: instead of saying 'Sun', 'Soup' and 'Sock', they are saying 'Dun', 'Doup' and 'Dock'. At home, you can try during your normal routines and dedicated playtime with your child to find words/items/activities that begin with the /s/ sound.

When out and about or shopping, you can look for all the things that begin with the /s/ sound. Emphasize the /s/ sound at the beginning of each word and you should say the word at least twice. For example: 'soup', 'seat', 'six', 'sad', 'salad', 'salt', 'same', 'sand', 'send' etc.

You can look at words that rhyme and see if your child can hear the difference. Can they generate rhyme words? For example, if your target sound is

Yasmin Akhtar

/t/, show them some pictures of things beginning with the /t/ sound ('tea', 'two', 'top', 'tap') and also have pictures that begin with the /k/ ('key', 'coo', 'cop', 'cap'). Put the pictures ('tea'/'key') in front of the child and you say one of the words ('Tea'), make sure your child can't see your mouth. Is your child able to identify the correct word just by listening? If not, try letting them see your mouth when you say the word.

Your speech therapist will practise and demonstrate this to you in clinic if they think this type of therapy is appropriate for your child. You will be given some resources related to your target sound to practise at home until your next appointment.

Syllable Clapping

This is something that adults rarely have to think about but it is fundamental for children to help them become aware of the structure of words and the chunks of sounds in them. It's good for children who miss out sounds of words and with practice, the goal is first for them to replace the missing sound with any sound, and then eventually the correct sound.

Just in case you need a quick refresh, here is a short sentence with the syllable claps:

Instead of clapping hands together, you can also clap one hand on top of the other or tap on the table. Some teachers in schools will also place their hand under their chin, and every time their chin touches their hand, it is a syllable. This is a good strategy if the child can't differentiate syllables by clapping. You might feel a little bit silly doing this but I bet you are trying it now!

Encourage Listening Skills

We have already mentioned the importance of listening and your child learning from your good example. As for listening strategies, there are a number of games that are great to engage your child in listening activities, such as 'Simon Says', 'Mother, May I?' and 'Red Light, Green Light'.

A listening walk is a great way to get children to tune into the sounds that we often miss. When you go for a walk, stop for a minute, close your eyes and together, think of the things that you can hear.

The TV can be your best friend or your worst enemy. There are a number of great programs that have been created with education in mind. To use the TV as a tool, it's important that you watch TV with your child and talk about the things you watch. You should also spend some time as a family with the TV turned off to reduce the auditory distractions in your little one's environment.

Developing Speech Sounds Awareness

A child needs to develop the ability to listen to and understand sounds in words, syllables and rhyme. This is very important for speech development. You can try the following strategies to help your child develop sound awareness:

- Syllable clapping

- Rhyme and sounds

- Sorting objects by the initial sound (all items beginning with the sound /b/: 'bottle', 'bricks', 'bat' etc)

- Copying sounds: Let the child be the teacher asking you the questions, getting the adult to copy sounds. You are obviously going to have to make mistakes and the child will have to help you say the correct sounds. This will help their learning, plus it will be fun that Mummy/Daddy are getting things wrong!!

Yasmin Akhtar

To help children identify which sounds are the same or different, we use minimal pairs. It is important to find out if your child's errors are related to their hearing. Can your child actually hear the sound they are unable to pronounce? You can play simple games to check this out. Your speech therapist may assess your child using minimal pairs and will demonstrate the strategies and provide resources for you to practise at home.

You can try the following to check if they can hear the sound. Have one pair of pictures in front of your child and have a piece of paper or your hand in front of your mouth. The aim is to make sure your child is only using their listening skills. Say one word, e.g. 'Tea.' If your child picks the correct picture, say, 'Good listening.' Now say 'Key.' If they get it right again, praise them and then say, 'Key' again. If they get right, then great. If they pick up 'Tea', that means they were guessing that you would say 'Tea' as you've just said 'Key'. It's a little bit like tricking your child; this is just to make sure they are able to hear what you are saying.

Key

Tea

Guard

Card

Pip

Zip

I appreciate that that was quite a lot to take in throughout this chapter. You may suspect one

Yasmin Akhtar

condition or various conditions, but any concerns should be brought up as soon as possible with your doctor. They will then be able to refer you to the right specialist, or team of specialists. Based on what the specialists say, you may start one of the many types of speech and language therapy with your little one. Remember, you won't do any harm by playing with your child and focusing on their speech and language.

Conclusion

First of all, I want to congratulate you and praise you for taking the time to read this book and educating yourself on how to be a better parent. So many children still slip through the system because of a lack of resources and support and I am so happy that yours isn't going to be one of them.

It's always going to be a worry when you suspect your child has a speech and language disorder. Hopefully, you have stopped blaming yourself and telling yourself off for not reading stories to a pregnant belly. Now is the time to start feeling positive because you have a massive range of strategies that you can literally start right now. I bet if you looked around the room you are sitting in, you could find at least 50 words that you could incorporate into fun activities that will stimulate communication. And the same can be said for everywhere you go.

The first step is for you to see these opportunities and not let them slip by. You might need to remind yourself every now and again and that's ok. After all, there are still plenty of other stresses and problems that tend to take over our mind. And, you don't need to go over the top either. Whatever you can do is going to make a positive difference, but try to dedicate five minutes a day with no other distractions, where you get down on the floor with them and let them lead playtime, so that you can observe and reinforce speech and language skills.

Another hope I have is that you will be feeling so positive and motivated that you will want to try everything that we have talked about. This is awesome, but don't overdo it. Young children have short attention spans and can tire easily. Even if it is still only playing, don't be offended if an activity lasts for only a few minutes before they move onto the next. Let them lead because as long as they are motivated, you can be there to help them.

You will notice that some therapies may have little impact and others significantly more. That being said, you won't see a difference in a day! Try to give therapy at least a couple of weeks for the improvements to be seen. Make notes of what you feel is helping and what isn't, so that as they get older, you can develop more activities along the same theme. The most important thing is never to give up and always have fun!

Your specialist team is going to become one of your strongest support networks and you should feel confident about reaching out to them with any concern you have. As I always say, no question is a stupid one! You can also reach out to me if you need additional speech and language support or a listening ear.

While the aim of this book is to help parents and carers who have children with speech and language disorders, I know that many other parents have also been able to use these games and activities as a way of creating a stronger bond with their little ones.

If you have found this book helpful, I would be beyond grateful if you could leave a review on Amazon. Your opinions matter not only to me but together, we can help other parents who might not be

Yasmin Akhtar

getting the help they need. Until the next time, good luck!

References

Agro, E. (2020, April 20). *Dyslexia and Speech & Language Therapy?* Mable Therapy. https://mabletherapy.com/2019/10/01/dyslexia-and-speech-therapy/

American Speech-Language-Hearing Association. (n.d.-a). *Childhood Apraxia of Speech*. ASHA. Retrieved June 20, 2021, from https://www.asha.org/public/speech/disorders/childhood-apraxia-of-speech/

American Speech-Language-Hearing Association. (n.d.-b). *Social Communication*. Www.Asha.Org. Retrieved June 20, 2021, from https://www.asha.org/public/speech/development/social-communication/

Yasmin Akhtar

Auditory Processing Disorder (for Parents) - Nemours KidsHealth. (n.d.). KidsHealth from Nemours. Retrieved June 20, 2021, from

https://kidshealth.org/en/parents/central-auditory.html

Bowen, C. (2016, June 1). *speech language therapy.* Speech-Language-Therapy.Com.

https://speech-language therapy.com/index.php?option=c om_content&view=article&id=47:input&catid=11:admin

Can Sign Language Help Children with Speech Delays? (2019, July 10). Speech And Language Kids.

https://www.speechandlanguagekids.com/using-sign-language/

CDC. (2021, May 17). *What developmental milestones is your 2-year-old reaching?* Centers for Disease Control and Prevention.

https://www.cdc.gov/ncbddd/actearly/milestones/milesto nes-2yr.html

Club, L. S. (2019, February 25). *Ten Reasons to Sing Nursery Rhymes; why you should be using them with your little one*. Little Signers Club. https://www.littlesignersclub.co.uk/ten-reasons-sing-nursery-rhymes-babies/

Cummins, K. (n.d.). *Verve Child Interaction - Keena Cummins*. Kennacummins.Co.Uk. Retrieved June 20, 2021, from http://www.keenacummins.co.uk/verve_child_interaction.html

Deaf Awareness Week 2019: Exploring British Sign Language and Makaton - Eureka! The National Children's Museum. (2019, May 9). Eureka! The National Children's Museum. https://www.eureka.org.uk/blog/deaf-awareness-week-2019-exploring-british-sign-language-and-makaton/

Yasmin Akhtar

Does My Child Need a Fort Myers Speech Therapist if His Speech is Hard to Understand? (2021, June 16). Focus Therapy. https://focusflorida.com/speech-therapy/why-children-with-down-syndrome-do-better-with-speech-therapy/

Early interaction. (n.d.). Helsingin Kaupunki. Retrieved June 20, 2021, from https://www.hel.fi/sote/perheentuki-en/0-1-year-olds/babys-signals-and-cry/early-interaction/

Early Intervention Research Group. (2019, May 20). *Using PCIT to Improve Language in Children with Hearing Loss.* Northwestern Early Intervention. https://ei.northwestern.edu/using-pcit-to-improve-language-in-children-with-hearing-loss

Factsheet: Intensive Interaction. (2004, March). Mencap.Org.Uk.

Speech Therapy for Kids

https://www.mencap.org.uk/sites/default/files/2016-11/Intensive%20Interraction%2004.pdf

Fingerspelling Game - 2 Minute Challenge. (2018, February 10). British Sign Language - Learn BSL Online. https://www.british-sign.co.uk/fingerspelling-game/

Firth, G. (n.d.). *Intensive Interaction: the Published Research Summaries Document.* Https://Www.Online.Autistipresov.Sk. https://www.online.autistipresov.sk/wp-content/uploads/2020/11/Intensive-Interaction-published_research_summaries_document_2016.pdf

Grommets. (n.d.). KidsHealth NZ. Retrieved June 20, 2021, from https://www.kidshealth.org.nz/grommets

Hearing Bc, S. A. (2014, May 22). *Language Delay/Disorder.* Speech and Hearing BC. https://speechandhearingbc.ca/public/disorders/disorder-listing/language-delaydisorder/

Yasmin Akhtar

Information about Acquired Speech Dyspraxia – East Sussex Healthcare NHS Trust. (n.d.). NHS East Sussex Healthcare. Retrieved June 20, 2021, from https://www.esht.nhs.uk/service/speech-and-language-therapy/patient-information-leaflets/information-about-acquired-speech-dyspraxia/

Introducing intensive interaction | The Psychologist. (2009, September). The British Psychology Society. https://thepsychologist.bps.org.uk/volume-22/edition-9/introducing-intensive-interaction

Johns Hopkins. (n.d.). *4 Common Pregnancy Complications.* Johns Hopkins Medicine. Retrieved June 20, 2021, from https://www.hopkinsmedicine.org/health/conditions-and-diseases/staying-healthy-during-pregnancy/4-common-pregnancy-complications

Makaton. (n.d.). Makaton.Org. https://makaton.org

Multilingualism: Empowering Individuals, Transforming Societies (MEITS). (2016, December 7). *Multilingualism: Empowering Individuals, Transforming Societies (MEITS).* Copyright (c) 2021 Multilingualism: Empowering Individuals, Transforming Societies (MEITS) All Rights Reserved. https://www.meits.org/blog/post/bilingualism-and-speech-and-language-disorders

National Down Syndrome Society. (2021a, January 4). *Speech & Language Therapy.* NDSS. https://www.ndss.org/resources/speech-language-therapy/

National Down Syndrome Society. (2021b, May 24). *What is Down Syndrome? | National Down Syndrome Society.* NDSS. https://www.ndss.org/about-down-syndrome/down-syndrome/

Yasmin Akhtar

NHS Lincolnshire Community Healthservices. (n.d.). *Opportunities to communicate :: Lincolnshire Community Health Services NHS Trust*. Https://Www.Lincolnshirecommunityhealthservices.Nhs. Uk. Retrieved June 20, 2021, from https://www.lincolnshirecommunityhealthservices.nhs.uk /our-services/childrens-services/childrens-therapy-services/first-call/means-reasons-and-opportunities/opportunities-communicate

NHS website. (2020, March 3). *Stammering*. Nhs.Uk. https://www.nhs.uk/conditions/stammering/

O'Sullivan, D. (2018, March 9). *LEGO® Therapy by Danielle O'Sullivan*. Sarah Buckley Therapies Ltd. https://www.sarahbuckleytherapies.co.uk/2018/02/lego-therapy.html

Reiter & Walsh. (2019, October 13). *Speech Delays and Language Disorders Caused by Birth Injuries like HIE.*

https://www.abclawcenters.com/practice-areas/types-of-birth-injuries/speech-delays-language-disorders/

Rudy, L. J. (2020, January 3). *Do Children With Autism Reach Developmental Milestones on Time?* Verywell Health.

https://www.verywellhealth.com/developmental-milestones-in-children-with-autism-4128725

SLT for Kids. (n.d.). *Lego therapy | Blog | SLT for Kids | Speech & Language Therapy, across Manchester & the North West.* Https://Sltforkids.Co.Uk/Blog. Retrieved June 20, 2021, from https://sltforkids.co.uk/blog/lego-therapy/

Yasmin Akhtar

Solomon, M. (2008, April 10). *The Effectiveness of Parent-Child Interaction Therapy for Families of Children on the Autism Spectrum.* Https://Www.Ncbi.Nlm.Nih.Gov. https://www.ncbi.nlm.nih.gov/pmc/articles/PMC5519301/

Speech Sound Errors. The most common speech errors a child is likely to make. (n.d.). Speechlanguage-Resources. Retrieved June 20, 2021, from http://www.speechlanguage-resources.com/speech-sound-errors.html

The Hanen Centre. (n.d.). *The Hanen Centre | Speech and Language Development for Children.* Www.Hanen.Org. Retrieved June 21, 2021, from http://www.hanen.org/Home.aspx

Turley, R. (2021, April 29). *10 Most Common Speech-Language Disorders | Online Speech-Language*

Pathology Graduate Degree Programs. Online Speech-Language Pathology Graduate Degree Programs | Your Guide to Communicative Science and Disorders Education.
https://www.speechpathologygraduateprograms.org/2018/01/10-most-common-speech-language-disorders/

What is Parent-Child Interaction Therapy? (2020, September 23). Kurtz Psychology.
https://www.kurtzpsychology.com/behavior-problems/what-is-parent-child-interaction-therapy/

When psychologists become builders | The Psychologist. (2012, August). The British Psychology Society. https://thepsychologist.bps.org.uk/volume-25/edition-8/when-psychologists-become-builders

Wikipedia contributors. (2021, April 24). *Intensive interaction.* Wikipedia.
https://en.wikipedia.org/wiki/Intensive_interaction

Printed in Great Britain
by Amazon